A GATHERING OF
GARTER
SNAKES

TEXT AND PHOTOGRAPHS BY
BIANCA LAVIES

DUTTON CHILDREN'S BOOKS

NEW YORK

ACKNOWLEDGMENTS
For sharing time and knowledge the author
wishes to thank:

Michael Aleksiuk, Ph.D.

Richard M. Meszler, Ph.D.
Department of Anatomy
Baltimore College of Dental Surgery
University of Maryland at Baltimore

Kenneth W. Stewart, Ph.D.
Department of Zoology
University of Manitoba

Library of Congress Cataloging-in-Publication Data

Lavies, Bianca.
A gathering of garter snakes / text and photographs by
Bianca Lavies. — 1st ed.
p.   cm.
Summary: Text and photographs depict the physical
characteristics, behavior, and life cycle of the red-sided
garter snake.
ISBN 0-525-45099-8
1. Thamnophis sirtalis — Juvenile literature.
[1. Garter snakes.   2. Snakes.]
I. Title.
QL666.0636L38   1993
597.96 — dc20   93-18932   CIP   AC

Published in the United States 1993 by
Dutton Children's Books,
a division of Penguin Books USA Inc.
375 Hudson Street, New York, New York 10014

Designed by Sylvia Frezzolini

Printed in Hong Kong   First edition

10 9 8 7 6 5 4 3 2 1

This book is dedicated to the memory of my pet garter snake Frederica.

Every spring in Manitoba, Canada, a wriggling, writhing carpet of snakes covers the bottom of a large pit. Thousands of red-sided garter snakes have spent the autumn and winter tucked away beneath the pit's rocky floor in a series of connecting limestone caverns. Now they are emerging from their winter sleep.

Common garter snakes always have communal dens, but a mass
hibernation like this occurs nowhere else in the world. Ten thousand or
more may be overwintering together, barely breathing, never eating,
until the snows melt and the warm temperatures arrive. The first snakes
surface in late April; they continue to come out until the end of May.

The red-sided garter snake feels smooth, not slimy, to the touch. Its body is covered with overlapping scales, or scutes, made of the same dry, sturdy material as human fingernails.

A type of common garter snake, the red-sided garter snake gets its name from the distinctive red spots that run next to a yellow stripe down each side of its eighteen-inch body. Like all North American garter snakes, it is not poisonous. It can strike and bite when threatened, but it is more usual for the red-sided garter snake to move quickly out of harm's way.

The snakes in this photograph are warming their bodies in the spring sunshine. Like lizards and turtles, snakes are reptiles, cold-blooded animals with no constant inner temperature. They bask in the sun or find some other source of heat to warm themselves and become active. In cold weather, they are sluggish; if it gets very cold, snakes and other reptiles must find protection, or they will freeze to death.

The interlake region of northern Canada provides a unique winter shelter for the red-sided garter snake. Hundreds of underground caverns, accessible through crevices in pit floors, offer the snakes protection from low temperatures, ground frost, and predators.

Not all red-sided garter snakes in the area spend the winter in the caverns. Some hibernate in other protected places, such as barns and basements—any spot where the temperature is above freezing. But most end up beneath the pits. There, come spring, the males and females do not need to go far to find mates.

The male snakes emerge from the caverns first. The females come out gradually and seem to head for the edges of the pit, as the one in the photograph at left is doing. Still sluggish from her long, chilly sleep, each female is pursued by a hundred or so sun-warmed males.

Soon rippling knots of snakes cover the bottom of the pit as instinct, triggered by higher temperatures, tells them it is time to mate. Only one male will actually mate with each female. After the male snake has implanted his sperm, her body produces a plug that prevents other males from inseminating her. The female snake also stops giving off the odor that makes her attractive to the males.

Females that attempt to leave the area before they have mated are followed by males. Here the males have pursued a female up a tree, forming a mating ball. The male snakes will stay near the pit until there are no more females to mate with.

During warm days in May, the pit is full of activity. But by the end of the month, it is empty. Where have the snakes gone?

They have begun their migration to marshes nearly ten miles away. There they will feed on the abundant supply of frogs, toads, and fish.

How the red-sided garter snakes find their way to the marshes is not fully understood. It is thought that most follow scent trails left by those ahead of them in the migration—but how do the lead snakes know where to go? By whatever means, year after year the snakes wriggle along the same routes, traveling through pastures, forests, swamps—and even small villages. Their journey takes them farther than any other type of garter snake is known to go.

The red-sided garter snake moves by contracting and expanding muscles inside its body. The sharp-edged underbelly scales catch and push against rough areas of the ground, propelling the snake forward in an S curve.

At top speed, red-sided garter snakes can slither about as fast as you can walk, but they usually move much more slowly. It takes most snakes about two weeks to travel to the marshes. Many do not survive the long trip. Some are run over by automobiles. Others fall prey to their natural enemies, such as crows, mice, and shrews. Still others have more unusual encounters.

In a town next to the pits, a dog named Kelly finds snakes, dead or alive, and deposits them on the front steps of the Lantern Café. Kelly's owner, Mrs. Eleanor Dombrosky, does not like snakes near her café one bit! She sweeps them down the steps with her broom. That is Kelly's cue to run off and collect more. He will be at his game for the month or so that the snakes pass through town.

But some of Mrs. Dombrosky's neighbors have a worse problem. "The snakes fall off the ceiling at night—into their beds!" she says.

Next door to the café, Mrs. Margaret Lillequist does not have a problem with snakes. She likes them. In fact, she prepares dinner while a red-sided garter snake she calls George looks on.

"George's tail was injured, and I painted it with white paint to stop it from bleeding," she says. "We feed him hamburger and fish. His favorite spot is near the stove, because it keeps him warm."

But George is not her only visitor. "We sit very still at night as the snakes come into the living room and play with each other on the carpet. When we arrived, the house was full of snakes, because it had been empty for five years. Once the previous owner moved out— because of the snakes—the snakes moved in! They must have thought the cellar made a nice hibernation cave," she says.

Despite the hazards of their journey, most of the red-sided garter snakes arrive safely at the marshes by mid-June. They are very hungry. They have not eaten for over nine months.

A red-sided garter snake's sense of smell leads it to food. It picks up odors with both its nostrils and its sticky, sensitive forked tongue. The tongue flicks in and out, transferring tiny scent molecules from the air and the ground to a special organ, called the Jacobson's organ, on the roof of the snake's mouth. Though it is not known exactly how, the Jacobson's organ can identify molecules left behind by different creatures. So a snake is able to recognize an enemy or find a mate or hunt a frog to eat. In addition, the scent cues picked up by this remarkable organ may help the snake find its way between the pits and the marshes.

Red-sided garter snakes are good swimmers. They move in water with the same wavy motion they use on land. The snake in the picture below has been startled from its swim by the photographer. In the water, it will catch prey with a quick sideways movement of its head. On land, it is able to strike, thrusting its head forward with jaws wide open to get a good grip.

Feeding on small fish, frogs, toads, and leeches, the snakes help maintain the balance of animal populations in the marshes.

This snake has struck and caught a frog. Small teeth that point inward toward the snake's throat help hold the struggling creature. How does the snake swallow the frog? It lifts up one side of its upper jaw, hitches it forward, then uses it to pull the frog backward as the other side of the upper jaw repeats the motion. Moving the two sides of the upper jaw alternately, the snake "walks" the food down its throat.

The red-sided garter snake can swallow a meal three times the width of its head, because its jaws are not fastened tightly together, the way ours are. They are linked by flexible ligaments and surrounded by elastic facial skin that stretches to accommodate the snake's prey.

You can see that the frog in this picture fills the snake's mouth. It blocks the air that would normally travel from the snake's nostrils in the roof of its mouth to the opening of its windpipe in the floor of its mouth. The windpipe leads to its single lung. Though the snake does not need to breathe as often as we do, it has a unique feature that enables it to take in air when its mouth is full. During the half an hour it will take to swallow a meal this size, the snake can thrust its windpipe forward, like a snorkel, for air, and then retract it so swallowing can continue.

As a snake eats, it grows. Its outer skin, which covers even its eyes, becomes too small. It must replace this layer of old, dead skin with a new one by shedding.

Ten days before shedding occurs, the old skin begins to separate from the new one hardening underneath. This separation gives the snake a dull color and makes it partially blind. The snake stops eating and is irritable. If threatened, it will strike rather than move away.

Just before the snake sheds, special glands secrete a lubricating fluid that helps the old skin peel off. Then the snake rubs its snout against a coarse surface to tear the skin. Catching on the rough ground as the snake moves forward, the loose skin peels back from the snake's body like a sock from your foot, coming off completely in about an hour.

In the photograph at right, a bright-bodied garter snake looks at the mask of its newly shed facial skin. It will shed once again before the summer is over.

In August, female red-sided garter snakes give birth to an average of fifteen live young. Here, a female watches as one of her babies is born. You can see the membrane sac that enclosed the young snake, along with a nourishing yolk, inside the mother. The thin, transparent sac provided an environment in which the baby snake could grow, allowing oxygen and moisture to pass to it from the mother's blood.

In the photograph at right, the newborn snake breaks through the sac to take its first breath of outside air.

Other species of snakes, especially those that live in warmer climates, usually lay eggs and slither away, leaving the young snakes to develop and hatch on their own. Although the western hognose snake and the smooth green snake do lay eggs in the Manitoba region, young that grow inside the mother have an advantage. During the cool Canadian summer, they benefit from the sunny spots their mother searches out for herself. When she basks in the sunlight, the baby snakes gain the warmth they need to develop.

Almost immediately after the garter snakes are born, they must fend for themselves. The mother does not bring them food or show them how to hunt. Their first year, the young snakes will feed on slugs, earthworms, leeches, and other invertebrates, animals without spines. Later they will add larger animals—frogs, toads, and fish—to their diet.

It takes the mother about an hour to give birth to all her young. Then she moves off in search of a meal.

Summer is almost over, and days in the food-abundant marshes grow shorter and colder. Too chilled in the cool early morning to move away from an intruder, this snake prepares to strike. Striking is one of the few actions it remains capable of in low temperatures.

While there are still a few warm hours in the day, the snakes begin their long journey back to the underground caverns that will shelter them from the cold ahead.

To study the red-sided garter snakes, scientists have marked them by removing a few scales from the underside of their bodies in a coded pattern. (This does not hurt the snakes or hinder their movement.) The scientists discovered that most snakes return to the same caverns they left in the spring. The newborn snakes, however, do not travel to the caverns their first autumn; they find their way there the following year. Where the young snakes hibernate their first year, how they eventually locate the caverns, and how the adult snakes find their original caverns are mysteries that still remain to be solved.

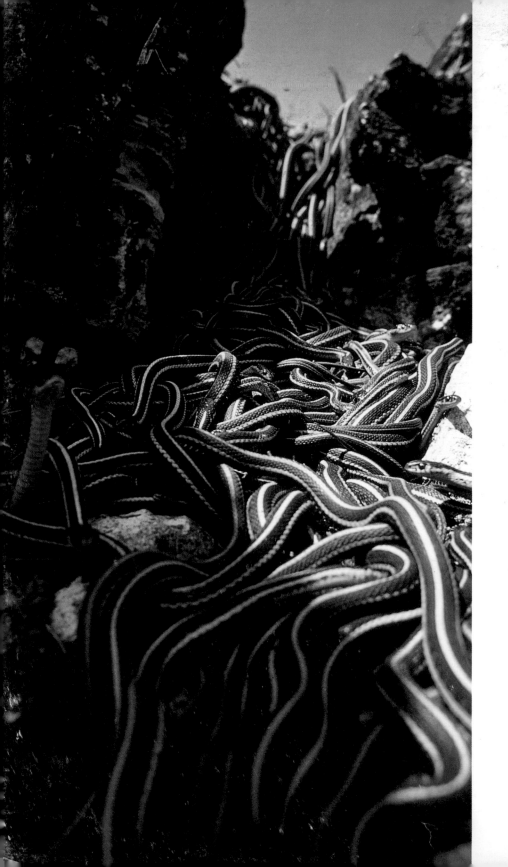

In September, the snakes arrive at their limestone pit. Soon it is as crowded as it was in May. Because of the cool weather, the snakes lie nearly motionless on the pit floor. As the outside temperature drops, they will slowly disappear through crevices, seeking the warmer cavern region. Their year will end as it began, in a long, protected mass sleep.

Some years ago, as more and more people learned about the snake pits, the red-sided garter snakes' very existence was threatened. Poachers caught thousands for their skins or to sell to laboratories and pet stores. In one instance, they used a bulldozer to open caverns, scooping up snakes and destroying sites for future hibernation. Now the Canadian government has outlawed the capture of snakes, and a wildlife management agency supervises tourists who come to see them. But illegal poachers are still a threat.

These remarkable snakes, which have adapted to survive the harshest natural conditions, deserve to be safe from human thoughtlessness and greed.

"I used to be terrified of snakes," says Bianca Lavies. "Then I flew to
Canada on an assignment to photograph the red-sided garter snake. Soon
I found out that as long as they were warm, so they could get away fast,
the snakes accepted me—as you can see here.

"I learned to accept them, too. I had to. They were everywhere. One
afternoon, when the sun was setting and it was getting chilly in the pit,
I decided I had worked long enough. It was time to go. I picked up my
cameras, still hot from the sun, and discovered bundles of snakes warming
themselves underneath. One snake had crawled inside the body of one of my
cameras. I had quite a time getting it out. Then, when I picked up my hat,
I found a knot of mating snakes inside.

"Driving back to the hotel, I stopped to photograph a sunset. I opened my
trunk to get my camera, and there was a snake! I put it in the ditch next to
the road. Later at the hotel, as I was unloading my gear from the car, I found
another snake, neatly curled up on the backseat, looking at me. It reminded
me of a purring cat, amazingly at ease and happy with the situation!

"I like snakes now."